ROCKS, GEMS AND MINERALS FOR KIDS

Facts, Photos and Fun
Children's Rock & Mineral Books Edition

SPEEDY
PUBLISHING

Speedy Publishing LLC
40 E. Main St. #1156
Newark, DE 19711
www.speedypublishing.com

Rocks are made of natural, nonliving chemical substances called minerals. About 50 of the 3,000 minerals found on Earth are prized as gemstones.

Limestone is a sedimentary rock that contains at least 50% calcium carbonate.

Limestone is often used in construction such as being added to paint as a thickening agent.

Granite forms when bits of quartz and feldspar are shot out of volcanoes.

Granite is considered the most abundant basement rock on the Earth. polished granite is used for countertops, flooring, etc.

Granite forms when bits of quartz and feldspar are shot out of volcanoes.

Granite is considered the most abundant basement rock on the Earth. polished granite is used for countertops, flooring, etc.

Marble is a type of limestone that forms when limestone is subjected to a lot of pressure over a long period of time.

Marble has been used to make statues and provide flooring since ancient times.

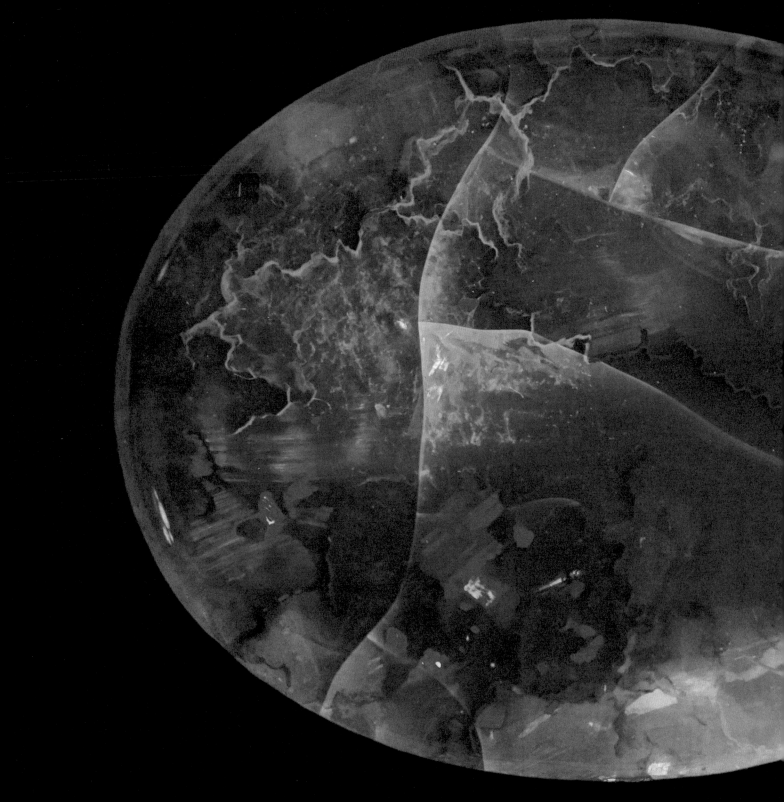

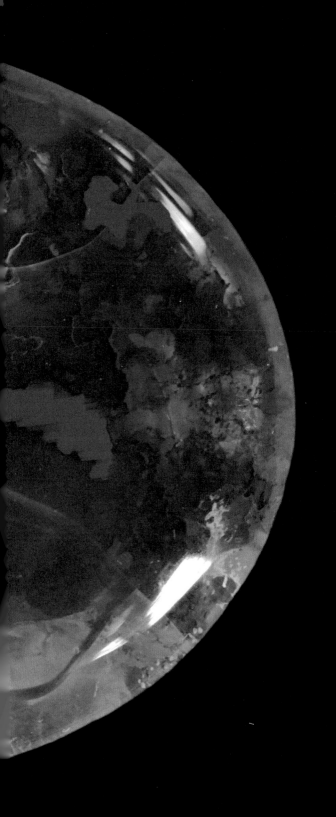

One of the most attractive gemstone in the world today is opal. Opal is often found near the crust of the earth.

Opals are
made from
tiny spheres
of silica and
lots of water.

Amethyst is one of the many varieties of quartz. It's beautiful color is caused by traces of iron, giving amethyst a range of colors from almost white to deep purple.

Amethyst gems have been used in jewelry and as a protective amulet.

Rubies are found in shades of red, from rich darkish red to pigeon blood red and pinkish red. Ruby gets its red coloring from trace amounts of chromium.

Simulated rubies were used in jewelry production. Rubies have been found all over the world.

Gold is the most malleable of the metals. Gold is mined on every continent except Antarctica.

Gold has
been used
for thousands
of years to
make jewelry
and coins.

Silver has the highest electrical conductivity of all the elements. Silver has long been valued as a precious metal.

Silver has been used for many years to make fine pieces of jewelry, coins, utensils and various pieces of art.

Copper is an essential nutrient to all living organisms. Pure copper is red-orange in color.

Copper is also an excellent conductor of electricity and is primarily used for electrical wiring and cable.